Easy Rock Instrumental Solos

Green Day

Kool and the Gang

Evanescence

Steam

Yael Naim

Bob Seger &
The Silver Bullet Band

Journey

The Rolling Stones

Santana
featuring Rob Thomas

Led Zeppelin

Eagles

Lifehouse

Arranged by Bill Galliford, Ethan Neuburg and Tod Edmondson

© 2009 Alfred Publishing Co., Inc.
All Rights Reserved. Printed in USA.

ISBN-10: 0-7390-5989-0
ISBN-13: 978-0-7390-5989-0

CONTENTS

BOULEVARD OF BROKEN DREAMS

Words by
BILLIE JOE

Music by
GREEN DAY

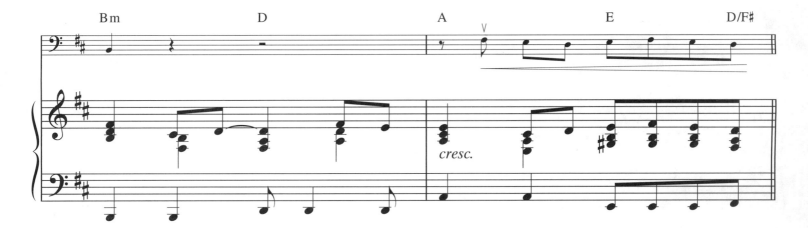

19 *Chorus:*

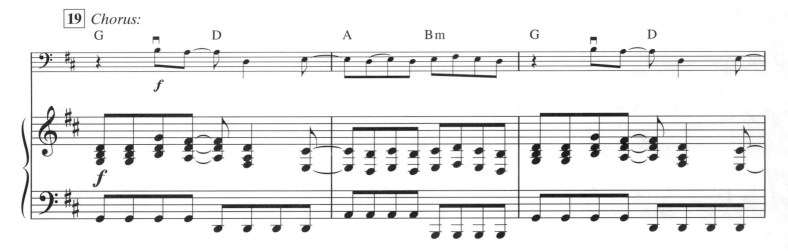

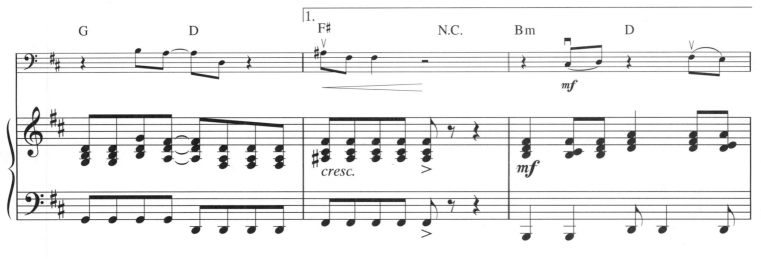

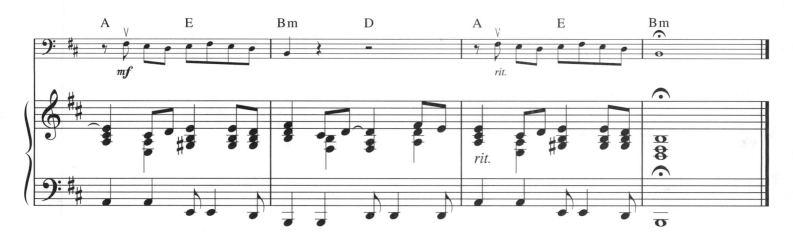

Boulevard of Broken Dreams - 3 - 3
32621

CELEBRATION

Words and Music by
RONALD BELL, CLAYDES SMITH,
GEORGE BROWN, JAMES TAYLOR,
ROBERT MICKENS, EARL TOON,
DENNIS THOMAS, ROBERT BELL
and EUMIR DEODATO

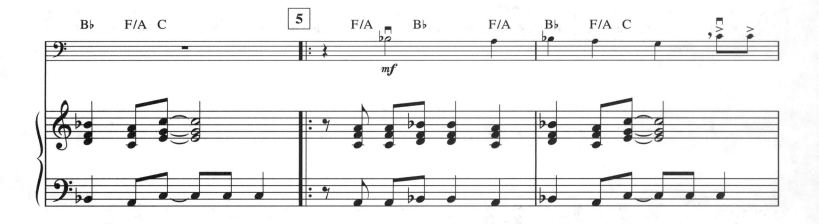

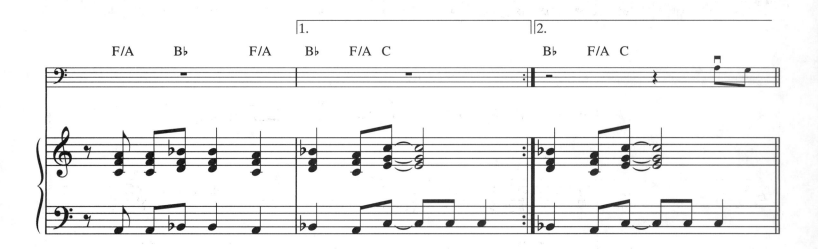

Celebration - 3 - 1
32621

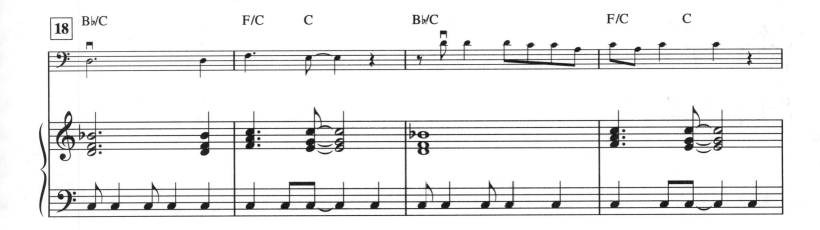

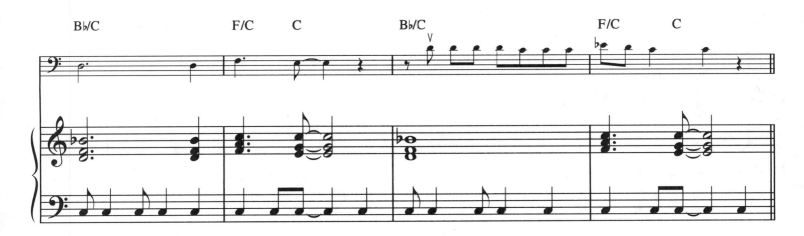

8

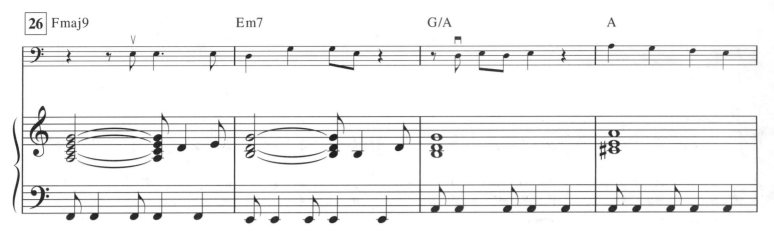

NA NA HEY HEY KISS HIM GOODBYE

Words and Music by
GARY DE CARLO, DALE FRASHUER
and PAUL LEKA

Moderate rock (♩ = 112)

Na Na Hey Hey Kiss Him Goodbye - 3 - 1
32621

24 *Chorus:*

Na Na Hey Hey Kiss Him Goodbye - 3 - 3
32621

MY IMMORTAL

Words and Music by
BEN MOODY, AMY LEE
and DAVID HODGES

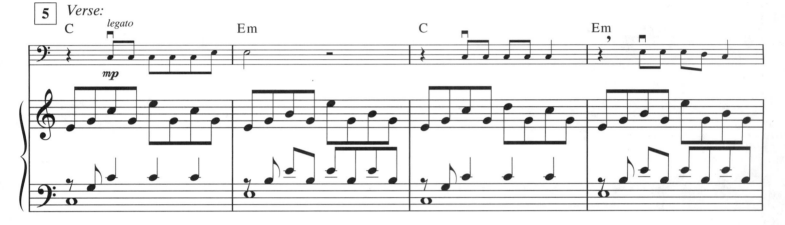

(with pedal)

My Immortal - 4 - 1
32621

17 *Chorus:*

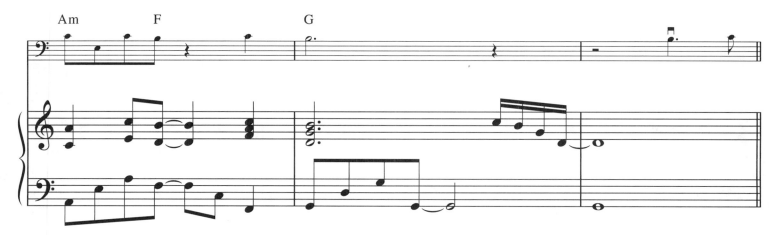

26 *Bridge:*

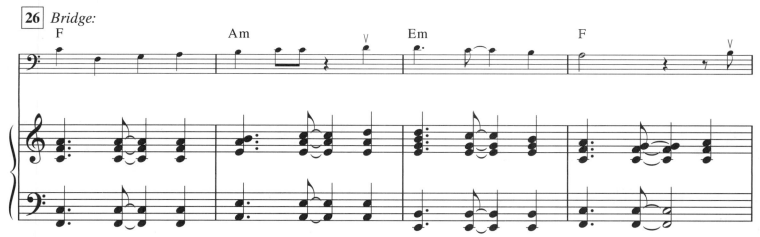

14

38 *Chorus:*

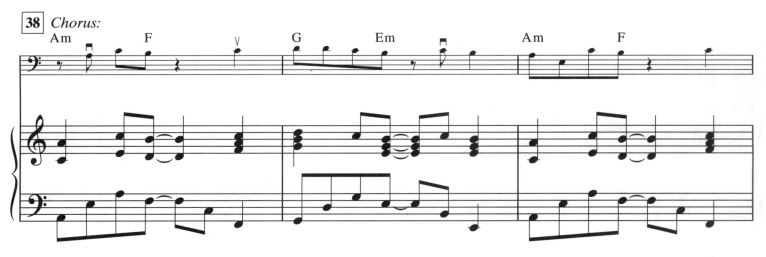

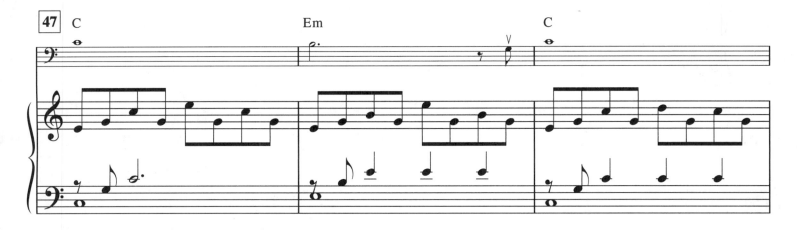

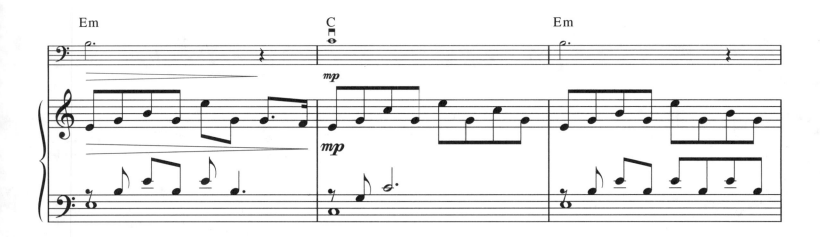

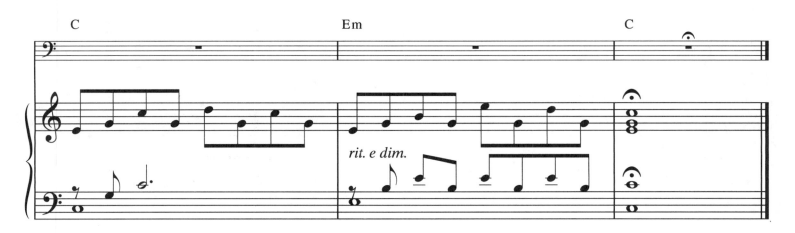

My Immortal - 4 - 4
32621

NEW SOUL

Words and Music by
YAEL NAIM and DAVID DONATIEN

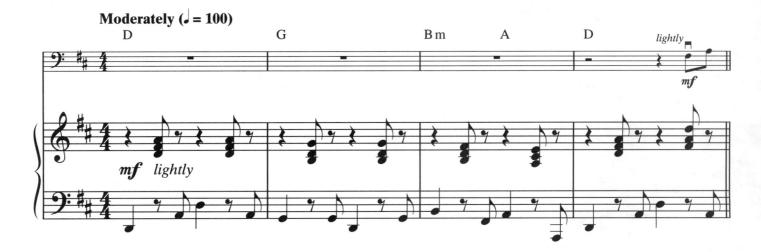

New Soul - 4 - 1
32621

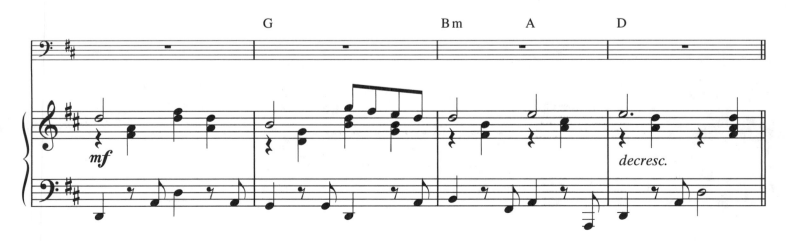

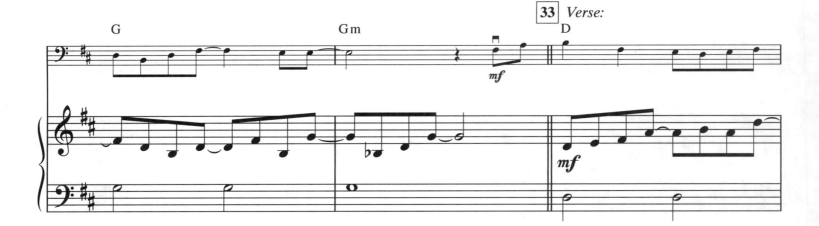

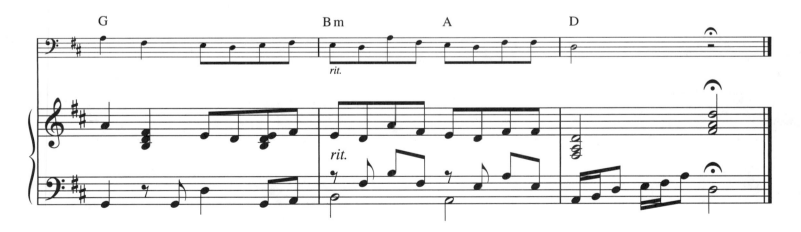

SMOOTH

Words and Music by
ITAAL SHUR and ROB THOMAS

Latin rock (♩ = 112)

5 *Verse:*

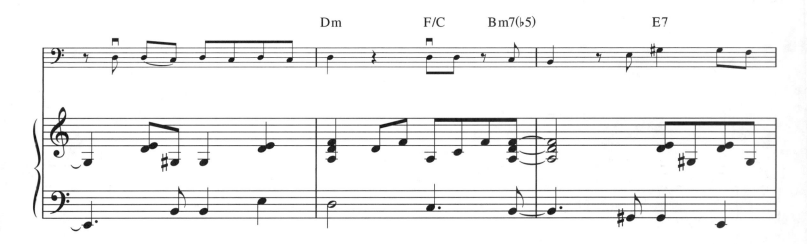

Smooth - 4 - 1
32621

31 *Chorus:*

OPEN ARMS

Words and Music by
JONATHAN CAIN and STEVE PERRY

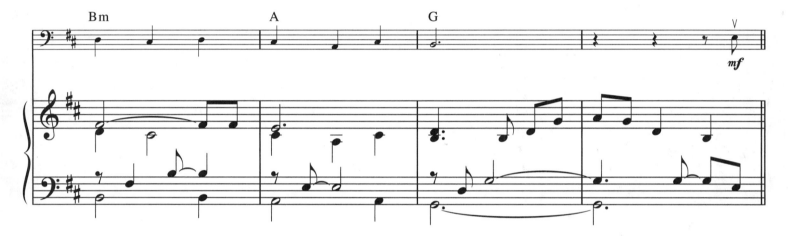

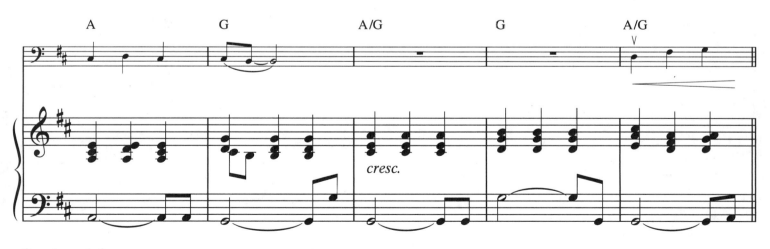

Open Arms - 4 - 2
32621

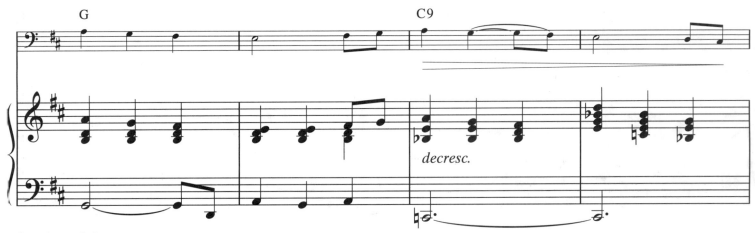

(I CAN'T GET NO) SATISFACTION

Words and Music by
MICK JAGGER and KEITH RICHARDS

Moderately, driving (♩ = 132)

(I Can't Get No) Satisfaction - 4 - 1
32621

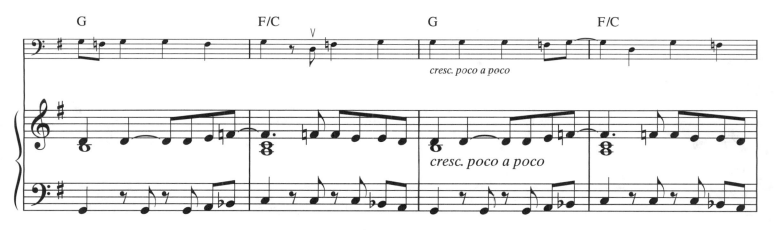

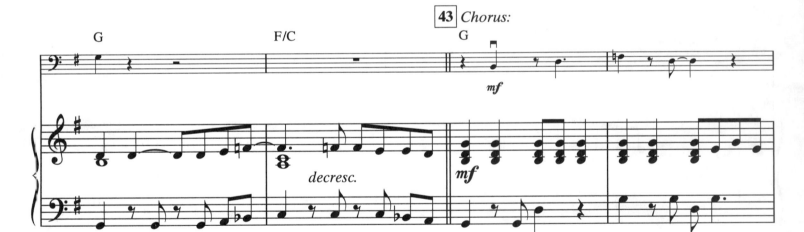

(I Can't Get No) Satisfaction - 4 - 4
32621

OLD TIME ROCK & ROLL

Words and Music by
GEORGE JACKSON and
THOMAS E. JONES III

Moderate rock and roll (♩ = 126)

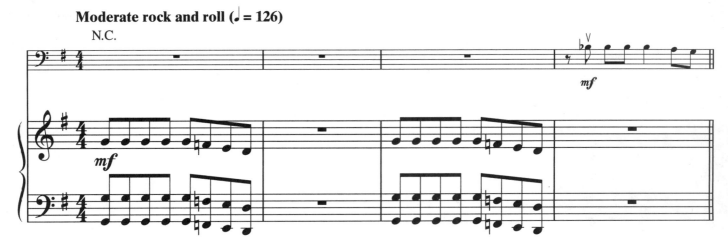

Old Time Rock & Roll - 3 - 1
32621

34

TAKE IT EASY

Words and Music by
JACKSON BROWNE and GLENN FREY

Take It Easy - 3 - 1
32621

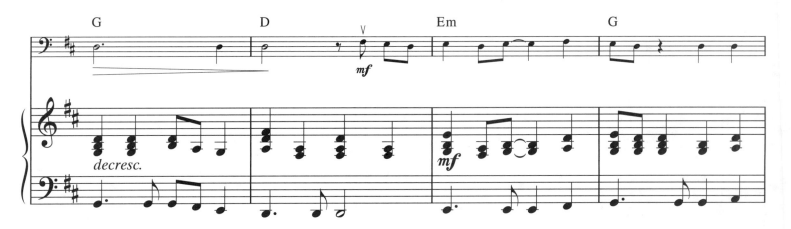

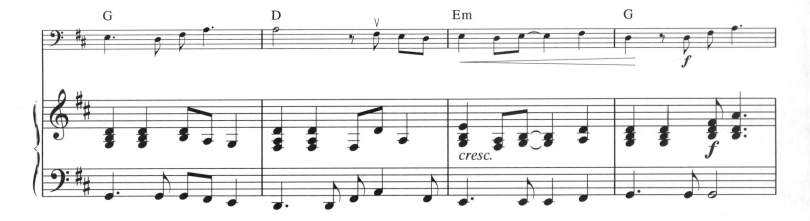

STAIRWAY TO HEAVEN

Words and Music by
JIMMY PAGE and ROBERT PLANT

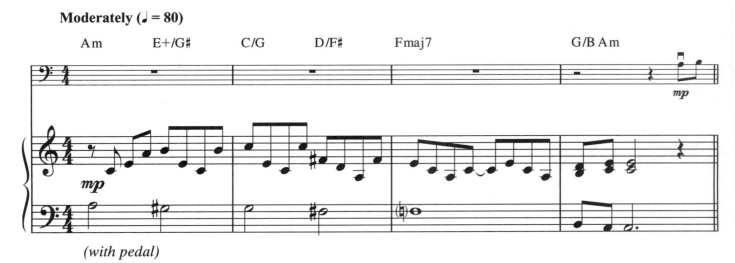

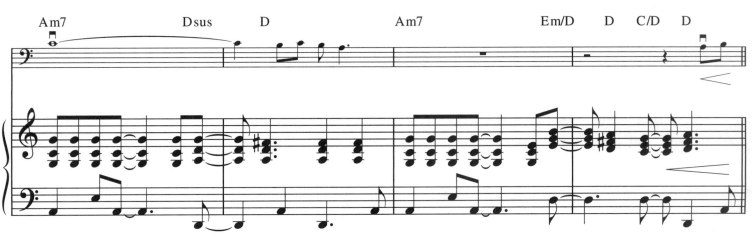

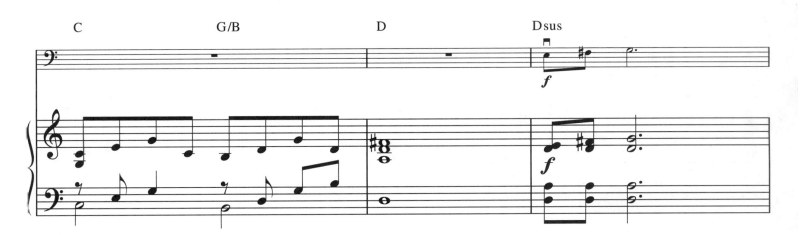

YOU AND ME

Words and Music by
JUDE COLE and JASON WADE

Moderately slow folk rock (♩ = 138)
(♩. = 48 This represents the song pulse feel counted in one)

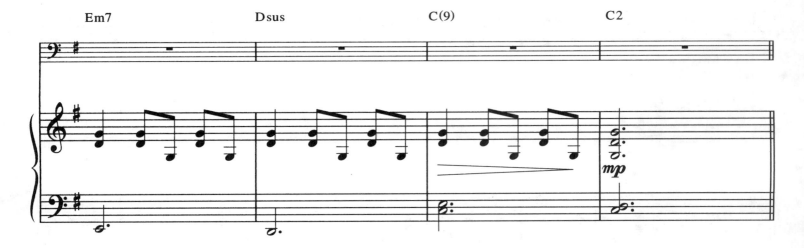

You and Me - 5 - 1
32621

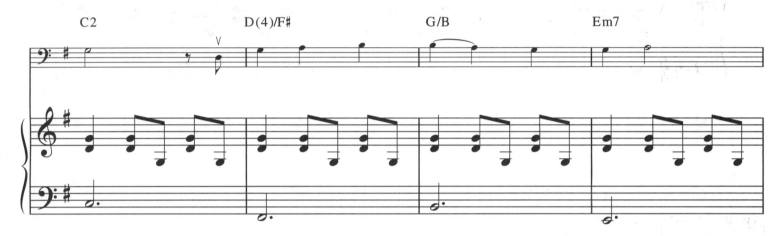

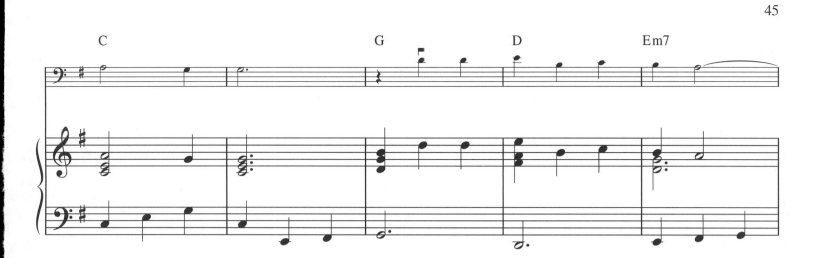

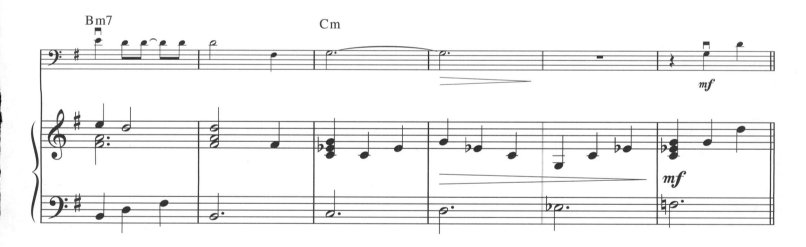

68 *Chorus:*